SHAKING THE QUICKSILVER POOL

other books by the author

POETRY
Dawn Visions
Burnt Heart/Ode to the War Dead
This Body of Black Light Gone Through the Diamond
The Desert is the Only Way Out
The Chronicles of Akhira
The Ramadan Sonnets
The Blind Beekeeper
Mars & Beyond
Laughing Buddha Weeping Sufi
Salt Prayers
Ramadan Sonnets (The Ecstatic Exchange revised edition)
Psalms for the Brokenhearted
I Imagine a Lion
Coattails of the Saint
Abdallah Jones and the Disappearing-Dust Caper
Love is a Letter Burning in a High Wind
The Flame of Transformation Turns to Light
Underwater Galaxies
The Music Space
Cooked Oranges
Through Rose Colored Glasses
Like When You Wave at a Train and the Train Hoots Back at You
In the Realm of Neither
The Fire Eater's Lunchbreak
Millennial Prognostications
You Open a Door and it's a Starry Night
Where Death Goes
Shaking the Quicksilver Pool

THEATER / THE FLOATING LOTUS MAGIC OPERA COMPANY
The Walls Are Running Blood
Bliss Apocalypse

PROSE
Zen Rock Gardening
The Little Book of Zen
Zen Wisdom

◆

SHAKING THE QUICKSILVER POOL

THE BOOK OF INFINITE BEAUTY

POEMS

February 4 – October 8, 2000

Daniel Abdal-Hayy Moore

The Ecstatic Exchange
2009
Philadelphia

Shaking the Quicksilver Pool
Copyright © 2009 Daniel Abdal-Hayy Moore
All rights reserved.
Printed in the United States of America

For quotes any longer than those for critical articles and reviews, contact:
The Ecstatic Exchange,
6470 Morris Park Road, Philadelphia, PA 19151-2403
email: abdalhayy@danielmoorepoetry.com

First Edition
ISBN: 978-0-578-01690-0 (paper)
Published by *The Ecstatic Exchange*,
6470 Morris Park Road, Philadelphia, PA 19151-2403

Also available from *The Ecstatic Exchange*:
Knocking from Inside, poems by Tiel Aisha Ansari

Cover collage by the author
Back cover photograph by Peter Sanders

DEDICATION

To
Shaykh ibn al-Habib
(and the continuation of the Habibiyya),
Shaykh Bawa Muhaiyuddeen,
all shuyukh of instruction and ma'arifa
and
Baji Tayyaba Khanum
of the unsounded depths

*The earth is not bereft
of Light*

CONTENTS

A Word About the Title   10
Reflection (*by Shaykh Muhammad ibn al-Habib*)   12

The Circus of Death   15
In the Glass on the Table   17
Scatter Ash   19
Branches of Knowledge   21
I'm More Concerned   23
The Man with Two Heads   25
Everyone is Someone   28
Little Owls   29
We Speak of Love   30
I Stood at a Wall   33
The Scaffolding   37
New York   42
Line Left Over from a Dream on the Train   45
Several End Things and Several Beginning Things   46
Circle   49
Rest Stop   50
Prayer of the Finches   52
Dialog Left Over from a Dream   54
Little Timmy Smith Smith   55
Death Sits   58
Salt Brine   63
A High Long Shadowless Song   64
The Saint's Achievement   66
God's Camera   68
For the Birds   71
Incandescence   73

How Love Happens   75
Words and Silence   77
Veracity   79
Bird Song   81
On Being Asked Advice by my Dearest Friend   83
Back from the Sea   85
On Second Thought   87
Story Out of Nowhere   89
The Sound of Earth's Rotation   101
The Puppets   103
The Prayer of the Angels   105
Some of the Heaven Element   106
Zigzag Road   108
The Fortieth   110
Tree of Life   112
The Wine of Life   114
Ancient City   116
In an Air of No Importance   117
Lightfingered Louie   119
Golden Globules   120
Non-Rhetorical Cat-Yowl   121
Phrases   123
Spectacular Sandwiches   125
Everything   127
Light Enters the Room   129
The Sky is Blue   134
Banquet   136
Angels Holding Small Mirrors   138
The Moment of Losing Consciousness   140
Dinner Bell   142
Shy Hemlocks Brash Niagaras   143

Ocean View   145
The Forbearance of Cats   146
A High Note   148
The Plum of the Moment   149
Sparks   151

A WORD ABOUT THE TITLE

It is said that at the Madinat al-Zahra Palace, built five miles from Cordoba, Spain, begun in the 10th century, there existed a pool filled with mercury, which reflected the sky and everything in it to utter perfection. It must have had a truly otherworldly shimmer. No doubt one would feel one was peering into the next world to look down into it, even seeing oneself in a new, more illumined light. As stated in various Spanish tourist guides, "Pools of mercury could be shaken to spray beams of reflected sunlight across marble walls and ceilings of gold…" Luxurious to the extreme, but also reflective of God's more infinite Beauty by means of a humble, finite human vehicle… a pool whose mirror any small breeze might make shimmer.

It also brings to mind the story in Mevlana Rumi's *Masnavi* of the Chinese and Greek artists who, to resolve a dispute between them as to which of them is the most accomplished, are challenged by the king to create murals on facing walls separated by a thick curtain, not to be revealed until they are completed, when the king should judge between them as to which deserves the highest honor. The two factions work night and day, the Chinese artists receiving all the most costly and exquisite colors they request from the king, the lapis lazulis and cobalts, alizarins and cadmiums, and the Greeks refusing any such materials to instead polish and polish their wall to a mirror sheen. When the time comes to unveil their respective works the Chinese artists present a sumptuous garden painted in meticulous detail, and no doubt unimaginably vibrant Technicolor. The king is beside himself. But when the curtain is pulled aside on the Greeks' wall, there's no image — instead a blank space spreads itself before him, perfectly reflective, and the king sees the Chinese image glowing with even more exquisite artistry, enhanced by the clarity of the Greeks' handiwork. The Greeks, Rumi goes on to say, are the Sufis, who have polished their hearts from all the rusty and dust-encrusted taints of the world, from all "lust and greed and hate and avarice," and he continues:

> The mirror's purity is like the heart's,
> receiving images beyond all number...
> ...
> No image is eternally reflected
> as one or many except within the heart...*

So, having begun this book as *The Book of Infinite Beauty*, but seeing such a title as a perhaps too easily misinterpreted boast, and hearing instead *Shaking the Quicksilver Pool* as more in the capacity of a human reflector of such beauty, the present title has stuck. After all, Infinite Beauty is an attribute applicable only to Allah, *al-Jamal*, Who creates everything out of love in a balance of Beauty and Majesty, two attributes sometimes clearly manifest, sometimes at odds with each other, as seen by our clouded fleshly perceptions. But behind every event and every creation is that *Infinite One*, and the quicksilver pool (imaged here) is perhaps evocative of our capacity to try to empty ourselves of our mortal *suchness* to the degree in which we both reflect and prayerfully embody His Beauty, and which, to bring our sleeping selves to life more intensely, we shake, we vivify, to see God's Face in the things we see... to animate ourselves for divine perception, now and forever.

To this end, I have begun this collection with my rendering of a poem from the Diwan of Shaykh Muhammad ibn al-Habib of Fez, may Allah be pleased with him, which is sung with heartfelt vigor by all his disciples and all those on the journey to their living Lord, entitled appropriately: *Reflection*.

April 12, 2009 – Philadelphia

---

*(Rumi, *Masnavi-ye Ma'navi*, Book One, lines 3500 [trans. Alan Williams])

REFLECTION
Tafakkur

by Shaykh Muhammad ibn al-Habib (may Allah be pleased with him)

Reflect upon the beauty of His artistry on land and sea
And journey through God's attributes both obvious and hidden

The greatest signs of God's limitless perfections are found
Within our souls and on the horizons spread across the world

Contemplate all physical forms and behold their structural beauties
In exquisite order like pearls threaded on a string

Journey through the mysteries of human languages and speech
That give voice to what's hidden deep within our hearts

Contemplate the mysteries of the body's flexible limbs
And how our hearts command them so often and so easily

As well as the mystery of how our hearts may turn obediently
But then fall back into creeping darkness and transgression

Journey through the earth with all its varieties of plant life
And note how vast are its flatlands and how many its steep ascents

Fathom the mysteries of all the oceans and their fishes
And their numberless waves held back by an unbreachable barrier

Note the mysteries of the winds and how they bring
Both misty fogs and rain clouds streaming down in drops

Travel through the mysteries of all the starry heavens –
The Throne the Footstool and the Spirit sent by God's Command

Then you will affirm God's Unity with the totality of your being
And turn away from illusion and vain doubt and all otherness

You will say, "Dear God, *You* are what I seek!
My impregnable refuge from wrongs injustices and deceit

You – my only Hope in answering all my needs
You – the One who saves me from every evil and every harm

You – the Compassionate One Who answers all who call
You – the wealth that provides the needy in their need

O Sublime One *to You* I raise my voice in prayer –
Hurry to me the Opening and the Secret O dear God

By the honor of that sublime one all our hopes depend on
On the Day of Distress when we're assembled at the Gathering

Upon him God's blessings as long as Gnostics journey
Through the lights of God's Essence in His every Self Revealing

And his People and Companions and all those who follow
The Divine Commandments by the sweet nobility of his Way.

(based on translations by Abdurrahman Fitzgerald and Aisha Bewley)

THE CIRCUS OF DEATH

There's a circus
the men all wear masks of death
you have to be dead to go

The horses are all made of flame
and rear up on their hind legs whinnying

The crowds are all dead yet they
look alive in their yellow suits

At the center is a black rose
the spotlight can't take its eye off the
black rose

The clowns are all sad
they wear sad expressions and carry
brooms
they try to sweep the spotlight into a pan
the pan turns into flying doves flapping under the
dark roof of the tent
but the clowns stay sad nevertheless

I want to go to this circus
and eat its popcorn and drink its
beer which turns its drinkers into
black roses

I want to watch its aerialists who
leap from their silver swings as they

turn into tigers

The tent is as big as all the heavens
the floor is as flat as all the earth
the elephants cannot fly but they
look at everyone with sad compassionate
faces and wriggle their sensitive
trunks

I see sunlit fields of corn and wheat
beyond the tent-flaps bathed in the
gold of day

I want to run from the circus of death
down the corn rows and wheat fields
and dive in the lake

and come out transformed into the
man I am
with horizons of blue light sprinkling in watery
drops off me

and the dark circus of death behind me

2/4

IN THE GLASS ON THE TABLE

In the glass on the table shone the mountain
in the glacial mirror on the mountainside
shone the sun and moon in their season
and the sky wrapped itself around them both
and at the core was the mountain
and at the mountain's base the glass

and you picked up the glass to drink and the
mountain shimmered
and as you tilted back your head
the sun and moon swam in their parameters
and as you swallowed

there was a new image aglow in the glass of the
curvature edge of things like a

blade slowly coming down that sliced the
mountain clean off its base and cut the
glass in two and left your
head as sun and moon enveloped in each
other's gaze your sunlight and your moonlight
entwined on the terrace where we

sat as you placed your hand around the
glass and I could see reflected in its water
the mountain its peak and beyond its

peak the sky in all its splendor
and your face like the sky in even

greater splendor in the

sunlight

2/6

SCATTER ASH

Scatter ash at the edge and let it drift
ash of the dead ash of the living
galaxial dust of our co-axial mortality
drifting among planetary spheres in tiny
flakes that once were smiles winks dinosaur tongues
palm trees around the last oasis for miles
perfect leaf forms in ash of exotic medicinal plants
floating in space for a million years before
alighting on similar plants light years away on
Planet Zagoz
(*love wished itself there and it came to pass*)
and onto the glowing

golden heads of its benign citizens like those
insect skaters that flash across the tensile
surface of a lake at dusk or even the darting shadow
of a dragonfly just as lightly skimming

Ash begins to fall in the perfect formations of
whatever forms they formerly were before turning to ash
ash leaf in detail to the tiniest veins and capillaries
lips that once kissed and were kissed by lips in return
ash preserving the forms of
everything floating slowly onto the
smooth golden brows of the Zagozites
who call themselves simply "the people"

They have waited long for this moment
yet totally misunderstand it when it comes

human ash lips look like nothing to them
ancient gem formations bottom-of-sea urchins *who knows?*

Eyelid ash that once drew down over the
First Dalai Lama's lucid eye
feathery ash remains of the first wing the first bird took wing on
long before the Pleistocene
ash floating here and now
drifting onto its destined landing place
like dust on a chalk board

treasure trove of our superlative mortality

jewels of our ever-fluctuating human intentions

fine ash flakes
fine dust you find on the undersides of things
dusty ash of our long sad mortal lives
happily immortalized by ash

ash at the very edge of things
ash of the living ash of the dead

2/7

BRANCHES OF KNOWLEDGE

Spillology
oleolography
the study of the way water flows over oil to make iridescence
spashology
zilography
the study of butterfly paths through the air and the
tacking patterns of sailboats
spansionology
zibberology
daggerish philentology
the study of gibberish
of insect nervousness
of the zigzag falling patterns of cloth
heartography
hingelology
smatteriography
the study of the subtle signals between lovers the
first week of their intimacy
smoothology
tenderology
all these delicate branches of knowledge
we need to encompass
encompassology
branchification
starlight how it mixes with dust
and falls onto us from way beyond what the eye can see
titeriology
splatterification
liquidology

*how rhythms of rainfall on concrete affect us
or its patterns down drainpipes or on
tar-paper roofs in shanty towns*

we go about the world noticing some things
ignoring some things sometimes to our
detriment sometimes to our
benefit the moon out the window as big as
all Texas suddenly craters more vivid than the
curvature of the earth coming right up to
meet us both sublime and
frightening

sparkleology
dazzleography
lunarization
happification
ecstasiology

or even just plain ecstasy

                                                                              2/14-17

I'M MORE CONCERNED

I'm more concerned
I'm more concerned he said
of how these next few years
these next few years will affect the small and

perishable things that dare to poke their
poke their heads up through the
permafrost that confronts us all that
confronts the big and small as we

battle against the very inertia that drowned
the unconcerned of Noah's time of the very old
time of Noah who very
successfully unsuccessfully built the

boat but failed to save his
people who were too busy being unimaginative though all
though all the signs were there for them
to see

the small and brave of us as well as the
big and strong

facing the wall of water
the mile-high wall of water that's just now on the
brink of cresting and rushing down with all its

absolutely every ounce of its impact wondering what
hit us

as if the earth itself were raised like a
wrecking ball and swung against itself

shattering the continents and splashing the
seas into space like a dog shaking itself

like a dog bounding onto the shore from a cascading
rush of water and
shaking itself dry

2/16

THE MAN WITH TWO HEADS

Once there was a man with two heads
they worked independently of each other and
everything went smoothly for the most part

one was named Robert and the other was named
Robert and though they resembled each other to the
swan-like eyebrows and cheekbones like
Mt. Rushmore and blue eyes that were
turquoise-brown in every light but green
there were significant differences

Moonlight falls on Robert's face while sleeping
he wakes behind a waterfall of blue moonlight

Sunlight discharges its golden rays on Robert's face
like bronze medallions tossed in the air and coming down
rain he is always in the picture
he is always in sharp focus while

Robert on the other hand is damp and wobbly
as if cut out of felt and
pressed against a low window

The rose tree survived his meek inheritance
sudden accelerations propelled the interior
Roberts ahead of their exteriors

They would discuss matters in matter-of-fact tones
under bridges or on rooftops in high wind

the two of them

Robert had a moustache and Robert had a moustache that
neither of them liked
*"Why don't you shave that dead
caterpillar off your lip?"*
The other snickered *"I'll be around
long before you're gone"*

The three of them two heads one body circumlocuted
every circumstance the world flashed by and
they saw no reason to come to even a
gentleman's agreement to disagree
or make any adjustment to co-exist in imperfect
harmony or come to simple terms with
things-as-they-are which is the
usual situation as we walk superstitiously under
ladders expecting the sky to fall on us Praise the
Lord Knock on wood
"Come in!" So

Robert and his namesake ceased speaking to each
other altogether and one would just let the
other order over-rich food or pay
too much at the department store or
say everything wrong with ecstatic self-
confidence thinking to himself *"It'll show him!"*
forgetting his own intimate connection for a
moment to the outcome

Robert's inner vision of himself was a

giraffe's head placidly picking fresh top leaves and
contentedly chewing green green in late
bronze African sunlight

Robert's other inner vision of himself or
other Robert's version of self (his) was
flagellant and flatter earth-flat elevator
up elevator down but never getting
definitively off at any floor for sure

It was a tertial complexity
complexification never-ending
this two-headed man who looked for all
intents and purposes as normal as a flea
yet two heads jutted from a polished collar
two hands gestured from two polished cuffs

He moved among us smiling-frowning happy-sad
sexy-sexless both in the identical instant

He sits in a hole and covers his head in the
dream this morning with monster cobwebs

He rapidly glides along tracks of slick iridescence in those
elusive thoughts you thought you'd never
think

Robert Robert
O Robert with two heads both named
Robert

2/23

EVERYONE IS SOMEONE

Everyone is someone which is
something we often forget

the deer with his antlers the slug and the
snail their little soft antenna eyes

ears on people hair on people
a volcano or moonlit lake in people

each of us a cosmos entirely revolving at
his or her pace

toward his or her death that envelopes
each of us differently pulls night's wool

down over us and tucks us in discriminately indiscriminately
counting each hair each regret each

joy each jubilation each occasional blank
space in between

across which we go boating with silent oars

2/25

LITTLE OWLS

Little owls
that lace the lumber of our dreams
your hoots astound us

those blinkless eyes two locomotives
out of the dark they blink and it's
over

when we wake you fly out into the light
as out of a barn door

O insubstantiality of all things

                                                                                2/25

WE SPEAK OF LOVE

We speak of love with words the size of fairy thimbles

as the dog next door barks through various
dimensions of reality at things *we* can't see
jinn on rampage
angels circling down in narrowing incandescent coils
onto wet black grass
fiery licks of flame shot from Hell straight up into
heaven enough to startle a mongrel and
make her howl insistent *outrage outrage outrage*
to make it vanish away so we can
go back to sleep again
under a purple sun

Night fastened down tight to its hills like the
flaps of a tent
the light behind such blackness waiting for its
chance to shine

Love is something you can't predict
yet it binds everything to a certain hectic nothingness
the way a season is bound to its weather
the way the sea is bound to its incessant waves

You turn your face to speak of love but we only see
the back of your head now
your words drifting up and away like fish bubbles
into the air

And the dark drama of the skies falls backwards though silver hoops
(*"Oblivion" also starts with an "O"*)

And people somehow leap their whole bodies through
their whole selves through hoop after hoop with
brave or tragic faces
tears on their cheeks or laughter

But love demands a new language
and won't wait for us to organize its
syrupy vowels and sly colliding consonants
before taking off on its own
down city streets and on the
sheep-filled hills of summer in a golden sun

I've seen it come in from the cold pulling on its gloves
for the perfect kill

I've seen it leave with no trace behind
while glasses unfill themselves of their most
potent elixirs

The dog next door has finished her howling and has presumably
gone to sleep like the rest of us

Love is the way all things in this room
keep from crashing into each other
yet all are connected
each outline touching
even ever so remotely

And the spider that let itself down
in front of my eyes today wanting to be let out

so I let it out

O my love

I let it out

                                                        3/1

I STOOD AT A WALL

I stood at a wall
there was no further to go

and hung oriental rugs on it
and intricate tapestries

glowed in elegant colorings
thick illustrious passages flat

before me on the wall
I could not pass through

and furnished that space with
taste and multiplicity

couches and tables of
burnished mahogany

and at the sides were vistas
and faraway landscapes

purple hills in the distance
but I had to face the wall

and no amount of camouflage
decoration could distract me

from the fact of the wall
which stretched for millenniums

before me
I can feel it in my heart

as I write this and I
don't know what to call it

wall of limited mortality
wall in our own selves that

doesn't stand there I could
pull all the carpets down and all the

intricate tapestries and clench my
fists and clench my jaw perhaps and

just walk on through it but once
I tried to *(or did I?)* and banged my

head face up against its brick heart
sore as if from love rebutted or

unrequited
wall

of imponderable nomenclature
not so easily undone

solid sitting there on your
foundations solid stone or

mortal mortar

birds fly across in sky-space

but we don't exist in sky-space
across the top of the wall unscaleable

you can see plain gulls or croaking
crows sail easily

I don't know what to call it
if I named it would it crumble?

Can I reach enough inside me to find
the perfect word to crack it

one perfect word or
string of words

but I still feel the heaviness so it
can't be this poem

the wall still looms there with
all its imponderability

God's wall I'm sure of it
just as God expects my stopping here

as well as my urgent urge to cross it
as well as my skeletal desire

to somehow walk through mortar
or stride through my mortality

with nothing in my hands
with nothing but the sky above me

with nothing to declare but Him
against the wall of perfect silence

that stands still there before me
wall that stands quite still

before me

    3/3

THE SCAFFOLDING

1

The scaffolding up around the building of insubstantiality
is made of human bones
a river of blood runs peacefully by over which is flung
a bridge of human sighs
and the sky all around is human eyeblinks
blue black blue black blue black blue black

Cries are heard from far away and near
shouts of human names and their replies
no one seems to be there but names are
floated as if they thought they were
someone must be running up to assume them
or else those oh-so particular names would
continue to float into space until they met some
celestial body that answers to Jeanette Rathbone
Robert Spring

A light rises up and filters through and also
sets behind the building of insubstantiality
made of all the human aspiration for complete
rest in the Face of God
complete release from fear
the heart made still though still beating

and all throughout this landscape and even
calmly thundering throughout the sky as well
is the sound of the human heartbeat

beneath and all around the building of insubstantiality
and all these things give it an almost substantial feel
but mustn't be mistaken for its utter transparency
through which God's doorway opens to let us in
to His close proximity
where real substantiality begins

The roses actual roses petals deeper red at the center
of human veins and capillaries
trees of spiraling light brighter at the roots
and yet of greater reality than any
redwood or sequoia seen growing by the
building of insubstantiality

and the roadway

and the arrival

2

A weak sun trickles through the window
like an English broth
dog next door barking again
clock on wall clicking instead of ticking
bedside alarm clock ticking
together they form a syncopated aural archway
Raven cat's asleep on chair by computer
someone's upstairs clicking on a light
foot treads foot treads tread tread tread
squeak of floorboards clack of cupboard doors

little by little the waking world builds up
from scratch
where the sleeping world is sunk into whole
muffled things half-seen
situations circumstances already in progress

You come upon
deer in a meadow chasing their hunter into a helicopter
while you stand wrapped in white bunting
reciting Yeats or up to your knees in eels

Floorboards above are squealing again
my wife getting ready for work dear thing
I'm down below like the troll under the bridge
in this world of addition and subtraction
multiplication and division
unlike the zero world beyond the grave
whose giant staircases can just be seen
hovering slightly in this pale soupy sunlight

and the roadway

and the arrival

3

And the roadway wrapped like a cummerbund
around this planet of insubstantiality
as it spins like a drunk at a party telling
tall impossible tales among the pictorial

configurations of the stars
archer lion balance centaur pistol water-carrier duck in flight
for the life of me
although our feet are planted in a trembly and irradiant
earth that goes on for miles whenever we try to
travel it as if it were imperfectly
flat so that you can understand those
nimble flat-earthers although their
imaginations lack space and sheer rotundity

Even so the elaborate long-bearded
hearts within us somehow travel with higher
speed accelerations and aren't confined by
mileages and street signs
and are themselves wrapped around a planet of
iridescent cascades rainfalls of tiny pagodas
and incandescent welcomes up
ivory staircases into high-arched doorways of pure ethereal sound

chimes hitting all the extra-auricular
registers with human voices breathing out every
name ever uttered and every phrase of
acceptance of our total godly consciousness
ever expanded or contracted among these
planetary star-lanes

Until we are indeed among the substantial
and all the insubstantial is blown away like
so much sand from a once
identifiable sand dune now changed shape

rose in black space deep red against pitch
blackness for miles including inner space

rose that by its pure redness turns absolutely
white as it opens and then
beyond white and even way beyond what we
think of as light to a
dimension of substantiality so far unknown to us
in which we will now proceed

God's elegance and sheer divinity
only hinted at by the cunning interknitting of
dragonfly over pond and butterfly migrations
and the deft way everything but us seems to
know exactly what to do in this life

and the roadway

and the arrival

3/4 - 8

NEW YORK

1

I'm in New York
sitting on the side of a rattan bed sixteen floors
up it's night in a March heat wave so the
window's open onto New York surf sound
illumined jeweled rectangles of windows in huge
office buildings some lit some not as if
signaling in Morse Code
indecipherable love messages
somewhere in the city a burning love is conflagrating
I hope it's on the ground floor or in
another world entirely so as
not to get trapped on a rooftop
there are identifiable sounds of motor vehicles accelerating way
down below in the street or
coming to a stop there's a kind of
stop and go to the sound itself and an unearthly surge
there's a strong human cry suddenly then
silence there's a kind of
voice above all articulating something just a
little beyond comprehensible but not quite
enough to be clear as if
leaning very close to a person dying to
hear her last words on
parched lips the spirit
struggling to separate and float
up between these ghostly tall buildings to
fly free

there's no tomorrow

time stands still

everyone's happy

2

I'm in New York
it's 5:30 in the afternoon I'm
sitting on the side of the same rattan
bed sixteen floors up while
all around down below growl various
machines of various sizes and calibers
car alarms going through their monotonous melodic
repertoire a steady
hum as if we're in the hold of a
Titanic on its maiden voyage
great engines churning deep under the sea line
huge gunnings of huge engines somewhere down in the street
brake-squeeze and churn
car-honk and oink
throbbing of movement so pervasive as to be almost
static
it's a roar that rises voluminously
a volcanic eruption of sound that ascends
bathes the being somehow lacerating
yet soothing right through both
physical and etheric bodies so that people
down on the street move with a

palpable rapidity in a forward moving stream
supercharged by the insistent throb
the all-encompassing growl

time is an endless river

the moment is forever

O grief O grief that
keeps us on our feet

                                                    3/14

LINE LEFT OVER FROM A DREAM ON THE TRAIN

She that has fake self-pity

SEVERAL END THINGS AND SEVERAL BEGINNING THINGS

Several end things and several beginning things
begin the whole thing
somewhere between ostrich feathers and a
blank checkbook
over the rooftops of heaven and below the Hudson River or
blood-tides and psyche-surges also that
run in floods
always arriving full of hope and vigor
eyes shining as if scanning a menu from God's own kitchen
overflowing with pearl soup and diamond roasts
goblets we drink that turn us into
glacial sunshine ponds on mountain peaks
puddle footprints of homeless
derelicts looking for a safe place to sleep who smell of
bad noodles

You come to me from the glittering sheepfold with empty arms but
news that exceeds my expectations

I see it in your eyes before it builds silver skyscrapers on your
tongue along a skyline of no human habitation

each pinpoint of a pin dropping in a silence perpendicular to
all the sounds the world makes

each gnat-jaw twitch or fly eye swiveling slightly to see
beyond the stained glass windows of its
usual field of vision

Joan of Arc seeing through the flames the
outlines of where she will soon be
celestial city where justice reigns with no
prevarication

Several end things and several beginning things
that we hardly notice the way they link and
weave together so seamlessly
the beginning's teeth clutching the end's tail between them
the end's teeth letting go of the end of the beginning
midway in the rocky road of life
glass windows reflecting us on the street if we
ourselves lack self-reflection
we rushing in coats putting on gloves for protection
as an ice flame goes up inside us or a
movie projection of the last 24 hours in which
endings and beginnings were getting all mixed up with
splice-ins from some obtuse angle altogether
beach stretching off to the right to a line of tall palm trees
cobras winding around them each with the
face of an acquaintance we might wish we'd
never made

There's no end to it and everything
comes to an end
there's no end in sight and
the end is always near

but cunningly zippered together end and beginning
so that even our deaths with all their
covering and wrapping all their eye-shutting and

anointing their carrying and burying
are not an end but a beginning
ermines instead of polyester diamonds instead of
plastic and a
steady diet from God's kitchen of delectable
tidbits and sweetmeats things
roasted in olive leaves or basted in a wine
that inebriates without drunkenness but actually
clarifies and clarifies

We see the far horizon disappear as if we're
on a yacht bound for Cathay
we see the near horizon open like it's about to
speak

We'll never get used to beginnings and
endings so smoothly dovetailing into each other
as we sail right into them as into a
sunrise twilight a glacial tropics a well-lit
midnight an enclosure that discloses
where everything bobs simultaneously around us
at last and where
only God holds the tight knot of
endings and beginnings hidden
in His Hand

3/23

CIRCLE

Who knows God
God knows

3/23

REST STOP

There's a framed colored print of an amaryllis
in this New Jersey rest stop surprisingly
sophisticated for a rest stop its
bulb and long leaves and open fluted white
flower with lavender stripes
in an overlit Roy Rogers staffed entirely by
Latinos so I got to speak Spanish to the
very Indian-looking guy behind the counter where the
various rows of variously unappetizing burgers are displayed to ask
if the egg-and-cheese one is available he tells me
"Only in the morning"
I say at eleven p.m. *"It's almost morning now"*
he laughs and I buy a
fish burger among a few strange other things before
hitting the road again with this pure
gorgeous amaryllis suspended in my
mind for a while before
fading like everything else though its
beauty fades slower from this life than say
the overlit Roy Rogers with its
various burgers these dark and beautiful
people so far away from home where everyone
knows and cares for everyone else I imagine and I
know it's fairly true
big families in various states of
poverty by American standards but in some ways more
vitally rich than rich Americans are with their
paranoid health premiums and complicated
fear of death

which hangs suspended in the air before us
like this amaryllis with its
white petals each with a lavender stripe coming
straight and strong from its central bulb
which is usually hidden underground in the
rich dark loam of our mortal longing

3/25

PRAYER OF THE FINCHES

The prayer of the finches
goldfish and things we can barely see
in watery element air or earth element even in
wood or iron

things whose minuteness doesn't prevent them in
any way from glorifying their Creator who's
cognizant and caring of each thing created no matter
if in horse spittle or on the Broadway stage

things of Baroque elegance for example deep undersea
of dazzling coral color or in the ether so
far out from earth's orbit they may be
many-headed or multiple-hearted for all we
know but if they draw breath or see through
eyes they also thank God they're alive with each
breath or eyeblink each
vista so golden or silvery that passes into their
view of planetary motion or orbital stillness

a song arising from every mite and termite
ant and elephant on earth or leaf in
mid-flight or having just
landed on or near a spicy tidbit fit for a
quick bite each time

the Creator is invoked beyond any
theological argument

each creature's magisterial heartbeat
in a throne room of natural splendor
looking out over valleys of sunrays

each bodily habitat a symmetrical garden
courtyard with splendid
exits and entrances a central

fountain spouting
emerald waters

                                                                  3/28

DIALOG LEFT OVER FROM A DREAM

Me: Mr. X you better get your coat
Mr. X: To fly on or to wear?
Me: To fly on
Mr. X: Well I'd better get it to wear it's a little
chilly out

LITTLE TIMMY SMITH-SMITH

Little Timmy Smith-Smith wants so much to be a train

Emily will be a great dancer one day
throwing herself off a balcony

James of Elfland thinks himself back in time
to when he was 2 inches tall keeping
dry in a squall under a grassblade

Harold of Lockley Hall thinks flight will
free him

Solomon Solomon will run three times round his
hut and still not see a tiger

Little Henrietta Hemmings will marry Timmy Smith-Smith
in Honolulu in a tacky hotel on the beach
they will swing and sway all night

Emily will have danced her last encore
seeing the handwriting in Edward's eyes
that corresponds to the voices in her ears
every tragic moment has a comic cast
one second too late or too early can cost
a life

We are never where we're not meant to be

Black Arrow Bart kept in a dungeon deep in

the castle keep until he is
skull and bones

Paisley Paul riding south on a London train
his hot lunch sealed in a box

Our paths cross or do not cross

We walk where forest creatures slid along
where our heads are were once where
whippoorwills whistled as they
darted by

Now space inhabits us the way bison inhabited
the Great Plains
and we launch ourselves out on it
to our peril or else
perish at the sidelines a perennial
pragmatist

Have I mentioned the long stairways going
up or the even longer ones going down

Little Bishop Penthorn got lost and nearly
drowned
had it not been for Benbo Pombo who caught him by the
sacristy as he was
rushing by

In all of this our hearts are either barred
or cozy dwelling places for the Divine

each as we go our merry way
catching a ride to Terry Town

where black night never visits
except on Tuesdays

3/31

DEATH SITS

1

Death sits in a transparent jacket behind the door
a hand reaches out to serve an exquisite wine
rodeo riders in tuxedos receive congratulatory urns
though their backs are broken and their
jaws wired together and their faces look more like the
cracked saddles they never use than faces

Death spooks most people by its unpredictability
though on some calendars the dates are
circled with humming bees that spin
round and round those sweet numbers
pollen dripping from their legs onto the fateful numerals

Furs around the collars of the wealthy on their
way to the Opera call to each other
silently by the silkiness and the present
stillness of their coats

A needle falls gradually through water
it falls even more slowly through glycerin
it barely falls at all through marble
though it might be measurable over a few
thousand eons

A neon sign blinks on and off at the funeral parlor
expecting more overnight guests than the local
motel

there's always a vacancy
and the beds are waiting though hard as rocks
and the phone doesn't call out
and the wakeup call confronts us
every moment

Whenever I'm stuck I write a poem about death
it gets me going though
I think we have to be taught to expect it
my consciousness now as I look out the train
window at the sunset behind April's
skeletal tree silhouettes has no
concern for its annihilation though the
sky darken over and the light blue get
sucked down into the horizon like the
Egyptian boat of Ra later scientific accuracy seems to have
replaced

Voices in the train corridor so cheerful and gay
saying their loquacious farewells
over the arches of the night sky
like a rich dinner getting consumed
oyster by oyster and asparagus tip by asparagus tip
the table gradually emptying and the guests
as we all are
gazing at a perfectly white cloth like an
icy moon over snow
with a cold wind blowing

2

For this section of the poem I was going to ask what
the angel of death might look like
then wildly speculate that the angel of death looks like
nothing we've ever seen before or even
imagined which is why we recognize him immediately and
take proper measures whatever they might be

or that the angel of death's like an
arctic shadow a trembling grass blade in a perfectly
still field or a face coming right up to
ours out of the air that is not how we have always
imagined we look like nor even what the
mirror tells us we look like but what we
actually and essentially look like so that we don't
see the angel of death as much as
melt into our own reality without thinking and
drift out over the open fields with it like a
low-hanging fog flecked with
yellowish edges

or a sound more than an image
so familiar and yet like nothing on this earth we've ever
heard before grinding tectonic plates undersea or the
sawing jaws of a Behemoth
so powerful whole mountain ranges are
devoured by it or all the

seas sucked dry by it

and yet surely that's not it
that's not the face of the angel of death

each person's own angel of death
the same for everyone down to the last hair yet

at the same time completely
different for each one

3

The bud that buries the stem in the blossom
surrounding it with a palladium of tinctured light
in petal form
stained windows

the big dead bug that lies at the ants' entrance an
inert intruder around which they
constantly must trudge on those
tip-toe legs of theirs

swallows' flight all the animated bird kingdom
carving a fragile calligraphy in the air
unread but by God's foreknowledge and
past knowledge of everything He's
written or will write for all eternity

I adjust my spectacles knowing He knows
and has it in His foreknowledge as well as His
past knowledge the exact date and

circumstance
my death would love to have fall as

gently and sweetly as the raindrops I hear now
outside continuously and sinuously

glittering down

4/5-9

SALT BRINE

The salt brine thrown up by a passing hull in lacy spray
is nothing compared to the peeling sky that reveals
a cataract of moving stone bearing
down on the island that moves aside for the

whale convoy sliding to open sea as the
cataract grinds its millstone ever closer to the

shore whole
bird flocks flattening in the sky the albatross the
poet's bird with tent-like wingspread upon whose
opening wings now all the sunlight in the
world alights as its slow wing-beats
cross into another world turning its majestic

head this way and that to let its cool eye cast a
beam upon this passing world
leaving it

nothing I have ever known or felt before
except in miniature

the world itself a shadow of itself

moisture and the living light
all that remains

4/10

A HIGH LONG SHADOWLESS SONG

How dare I write poems called Infinite Beauty
and they're all about death that blue-faced
yellow-fingered spook who rides the trains one
seat behind us

how can that be infinite beauty?

We walk under linden trees in blossom under
oriental cherry trees exploding tiny pink universes
we walk between oaks where crows alight
between elms full of sparrows
we walk to the edge of the world where whales wash
by lifting themselves up out of watery deeps and then
plunge back in again so barnacles and whatnot break off
we walk on the moon in an eerie
chalky light and there's old

death as always like a shadow rippling happily across
crater ridges or even linden shadows
shadow across shadow slipping
shadow sliding out of shadow ever so subtly
shadow swallowed by shadow finally entirely
and we too are mere shadows eating sushi
chewing slowly with dancing eyes above our mouths' dark alcoves
we are articulate shadows eloquently gesturing
out of ourselves to other shadows
we are mere shadows of our former selves
which were robust clearly defined angelically
inspired wisdom seekers and wisdom dispensers

in a state of perfect grace not only in
Eden but walking around God's Face clearly
visible in all things in our hearts

Now we drag along reciting the
International Constitution of the State of Uncertainty
like shadows putting on face makeup with
lots of blush and skin tone

But it doesn't really fool anyone
we sing a shadowy song and wear a
shadowy expression in our eyes
unless we see through shadow to the
clear green Land Beyond

where our eyes glitter
and our hearts lose their shadows like someone
taking off gloves

to sing instead
a high long

shadowless song

4/17

THE SAINT'S ACHIEVEMENT

When the saint reached his goal
only a chipmunk took notice
all that light pouring out of his room like a
private aurora borealis just for
Him
and scampered home to tell his wife and kids

For a split second the universe stood still from its
usual flipping back and forth from
existence to non-existence and took a quick
look at itself in the mirror of wonder and wondered
if all its lakes would evaporate all its
peaks eventually crumble all its
tombs keep their tenants cozy until time to
unfold like a magnolia bud into flower

Then it was back to business as usual and ten-times
greater radius of illumination around his head
which later worker ants took notice of and
passed along the grapevine
waterfall water cascading at its usual
pleasure babies getting born in sterile
hospitals at their usual rate

while like a newborn deer our saint ecstatically
stumbling in fields of God's glory like so many
sparks from a campfire meeting at the
pinnacle of night or the transformation from a
large top-heavy and earthbound thing to something

suddenly aerial and gliding
free

our friend gravity becoming here now the
dance master of the spirit's freedom from it
our saint's happy stuttering across a very
anti-gravitational threshold in order to
appear to us perfectly normal
saying perfecting normal things such as

Those are roses those are thorns

The night on its double axle turns

*The forward depends on the backward to
define its place*

*Our life is a split-second of joy before
light descends*

                                                      4/22

GOD'S CAMERA

If I had all the pictures in the roll developed I wonder
if it would show the light through the jeweled
stained glass in all its
cobalt blues and ruby reds that says *I love you* would it

show the disappearing clouds of antelope who can
change direction on a dime as they scamper up a
hill or cross an open space especially if they smell
lion in the air or suddenly in some deep unfathomable
animal way of theirs remember to go
back the way they came as if out of the
blue with all that
open space before them closing up more
narrowly behind them

and so I do love you though it may go uncaptured
great propeller blades go round and round but
out of the picture and the great unspeakable
body of it lifts off and into the night with only the
faintest light to navigate by dangling ahead of
us and it seems we put the

light like a carrot out before us to draw us
forward over uncharted territories where a
patchwork of lights and shadows almost spells out a
secret meaning meant only for us but then turns out to be
mere chiaroscuro of the normal sort although
nonetheless miraculous
none of which shows up on the film's emulsion

since only so much can be transcribed by
physical light so much darkness so much love
unspeakable indescribable totally out of the frame

the play of nostrils taking in air
the eyes' dazzlement the mind's defeat before the
actual outcome of the exact puzzle pieces of
fate fitting so snugly together
and the way perfection keeps falling into place then
falling into place again
again and again seamlessly

the tattered pieces coming apart then joining again
not on the film though I develop it
over and over to blow up each print to catch
details lost on the casual beholder
the casual beholder basically losing so
many of the details etched so deeply in our
hearts of the winding ways inward and
windward that unravel our story in its
deepmost subtlety forward

and you come into focus your face and your
form and it's mountains and sky and a
cloud sailing over that perfectly punctuates it all
before it dissolves away even the oldest and almost
prehistoric aspects of this
time and place held together not by a mere
picture of it but by a breath or something so
ineffably light as to be almost
evanescent as light itself as it

flows out of sight as it

goes forward advancing as a
film advances on a
camera that can't even
catch it as it goes only

God's camera catching it

                                                                    4/26

FOR THE BIRDS

All God's universes are bending toward God's earth this morning
to listen to the chorus of birds waking

up from their various branches and night-haunts
chirping syncopatedly in little

bursts as the mist-gray sky turns bluer
and our lives also look around from their

various nests and perches attempting to sing
waves and ripples of birdsong like small

chugging machines designed by Paul Klee or at least
perky with mystical delicacy and the

colors of mystery
deep rose mauve ochre purple dark green solitudes of

dream or visionary landscapes with silver
lakes floating just above the surface

casting deep black shadows on the ground passing
slowly as clouds

full of birds chirruping passengers in a blimp
cruising slowly over the earth feathery heads cocked from

side to side to sightsee through their little
beady black birds' eyes as they pass

silent for a moment over grandiose sights like the
Grand Canyon then suddenly

noisy again as they fly into its depths hurling themselves down on
splashing arcs of song since they're

birds after all not passengers in a blimp
ecstatic messengers from God's Eternal Land of Silence

spraying splattering arias of joyous noise
into our own

5/5

INCANDESCENCE

Incandescence at the hoof and forelock
incandescence that twirls at the end of a rope
and lights up expressions on faces of strangers
under black branches of a silhouette tree
tree of night and death tree of fortitude and
ultimate incandescence

Somehow everything begins in darkness and
ends in incandescence
while the middle is distraction and
gestures youthful
attitudes and experimentation watching the
last bison hunched toward annihilation
looming bulks like whales undersea
blank faces working black tongues in their mouths over
wet grass thoughtfully

I await the next dictation
the horn doesn't sound until it's raised to
incandescent lips
and sweet notes blown

and if there is no sound
soundlessness is the sound
and if there is no light
darkness is the light

God hasn't blessed matter with
anything but itself

incandescent spirals at the
center of everything

5/6

HOW LOVE HAPPENS

How love happens
a kite of white almost translucent wings
suddenly bangs into view in a
blue cloudless sky pulling at its single string to let
air currents carry it where they will
battered to death out of view
balsa struts and tissue paper panels dissolving like
spun sugar in the higher atmospheres
until there is only blue sky again

But the event you say the event of love
comes from the side
shot up like a shock a geyser of gold sparks
slender apprehensions become major
intimations where desire is pounded into
churning massive shapes

The event which is our battered hearts taking in
blood where the legendary phoenix boiled in flames
is born a tiny replica that grows as it flies
beyond the size of albatross or eagle
blotting out the sky
wings on fire fanned by flight into a major conflagration
dissolving in the sky at last like the kite of the first stanza

and other things rise through the living solution of love
released from the surface as bubbles that
rise in the air then dissolve in the air
like the kite of the first stanza and the phoenix of the third

and the dissolving world in which these various
stanzas boil into a froth and become animated

love writing itself letters it kisses and folds away into love's deep
pockets
not knowing what else to do

then gazes out through the forest
listening to earliest birds
also sing of love

5/9

WORDS AND SILENCE

Anguish (but in French it's "*angoisse*"
which seems to have more
anguish as a word)
came over the mountain and *Pity* and
Anger dressed in black with pitchforks
and some of the dreamier words like
Care and *Disposition* in swathes of tulle
also trooped gamely over the mountain and
down into the valley where other cousins of
these words were already waiting some with
droopy mountain mustaches others already
listening to cell phones or dialing and
waiting for an answer

The sun was reaching its noon apex and the
words were sweating a little wondering
why they'd been called together had they been
lax or failed in their jobs
were they being retired from service
as had a horde of words only a year before
some now working as domestics in nearby
villages where the people don't even speak the same
language some opening small thrift shops or
selling fire wood by the road
none doing better than they had when in full
use in speech between people
now hoping for a better day
when they'll be called back into more than
lip service

As time wore on more and more words congregated

words like *Congregated Contraption Anticipation Fool's Gold*
none knew why they were being assembled
until at last the crowd gave way and
silence rode in on a pure white horse her gold hair
hanging down over her nakedness
her bronze skin reflecting the now high afternoon sun
her turquoise eyes aglitter

She rode to the center of the crowd
no one dared speak she pushed her hair aside and
disappeared the words also like water in a
drain suddenly whirled in diminishing circles round and round
and entered complete silence

until the field was empty
except for the white horse with incipient
wings that bent down its wonderful sleek

silvery neck and grazed on the verbiage

5/10

VERACITY

I wonder if I saw Martians anyone would believe me or if I
saw a truly marvelous sight like a
cosmos coming to birth in the clouds as an
exploding egg of redness blown to incandescent heat then
released as revolving planets and moons and even
stars in perfect order throughout chaotic snap and
twist of placement in a background of the
heavens or in the cupped
palm of my hand or the birth of a

wingéd horse from a loaf of bread or a trooping of
fairies from under a downed
tree trunk in the woods during my regular morning
walk the way I saw
Marilyn Monroe right next to me in a crosswalk in
San Francisco going the opposite direction incognito in
dark glasses and nondescript clothes shorter than my height
five-feet-ten (she was actually five-feet-five and a half),
but I knew immediately and instinctively it was
her without makeup and washed-out blond hair rather
unkempt looking down at her feet as she
walked I
knew it was Marilyn though no one else seemed to
notice I wonder if I saw

the end of the world like a cinematic preview hurled up on
the insides of giant atmospheric breakers in the
sky people would believe me if I was the
only one and no one else had

witnessed it and of course
why should they why should anyone believe
anything anyone says unless we have an
absolutely spotless record and are
corroborated as such by handfuls of people the way
the Prophet was God bless him or any of the
prophets who were of course generally
disbelieved and mocked thrown out by their
own people and disavowed though on the
inside of the eyelids of their worlds
clarity threw pictures in perfect focus and
Divine Dimensions absolute decisiveness
later unassuaged unassailable truth told in
plain extraordinary speech

Or if one day I saw out of the wall come
a new race of people to take
over from our own people of vision and benignity

people utterly benign of
perfect dignity

5/12

BIRDSONG

In a moment he was surrounded by a
million birds

the contours of his head gave way
the mind's boundaries and he was flooded

with birdsong transported on
nothing more than liquid notes in

quick succession up and down a scale deliciously
intrinsic only to birds

He lost his footing in such a gush of sound
gained head plumage and a certain

lightness and hardness both (beak brittle
eyes fierce and beady)

flying off at an acute angle to the earth
though never leaving ground never really

taking to the skies except in
the clear consciousness of doing so

The multiplicities of song not mute of meaning while being
strong of sound though not of a language one could

learn and reproduce
their song to them like bark to trees

like grass on plains to the plains themselves
their song like wings to birds

out of heaven sibilant drops
cascading down

filling him
surrounding him

　　　　　　　　　　　　　　　　　　　　5/13

ON BEING ASKED MY ADVICE BY MY DEAREST FRIEND

for Hakim Archuletta

What I know couldn't dye
one side of a microscopic thread floating in space

What I *don't* know could propel every
gushing river even faster down its
cascades into steaming froth the sound
drowning out every other earthly sound

What I know wouldn't influence a single
gnat in midair over the Sahara to go one
micrometer of a hair to the right or left without any
obstacle in all directions for a million miles

What I *don't* know accompanies
in empathetic rhythm
the breathing patterns of every
living creature at this very moment on this
very planet every inbreath every
outbreath down to the tiniest mouse as well as the
grandest elephant taking his ease hosing loose
dust on his back to cool off in the
African sun

What I know would be ignored by most of the
solar system in its graceful swirl in space

What I *don't* know could be even that much more completely
ignored to the point that neither
one nor the other would ever be entertained for even a
billionth part of a nanosecond in this
great universe's mental workings

Though what I do know now that I
think of it might be at least the paradisiacal
nervous impulses that run up and down through my
happily God-given being body and soul for all
eternity amen

While what I *don't* know
the sum and music of it all
would definitely be the glorious
flood of all things

in which all things

including every God-given being

flow

5/16

BACK FROM THE SEA

Back from the sea back from the
   tumultuous sea
a sailor with one leg one eye one hope in the
world to live his life before dying

He has a map he puts his head on to sleep
he has a long bone and a short nail he
arranges in a mystic pattern when he wakes
strange tattoos from Tahiti
tales to tell of great escapes

The world doesn't fall off where sky meets horizon
a green glimmer over the waters often writhed itself into
singing mermaid shapes
a strange white light occasionally wrapped itself around the mast
stillness often overtook the ship the crew the
waves the stars the whole earth stood on
one toe over the sky casting no shadow

Light spelled out his name on his birthday at sea
the angles of the floor the seesaw of the floor
made a nimble dancer of him
made him walk like a dancer on solid ground
made him think like a dancer long after there was
rolling water under him
solitary gymnast lone negotiator of gravity's
vagaries

He saw the moon one night split in two

he saw angels fill the sky with their faces flat above looking
down holding him in their eyes and singing

He sat at a table years later telling this to no one
in a solitary room on earth as the
whole earth's rolling tide turned him slowly
round and round

And the stars around him on all sides and even
under him mapped out his lone position in
relation to them
pinpointing his soul's longitude and latitude to the
first degree

This brave sailor

This lone sailor back from the sea

5/20

ON SECOND THOUGHT

On second thought
the tall stalk of the single-trunked tree sprang
actually sprang full-grown from a green clump
laughter filled the tunnel

On second thought something gave way and the whole
apparatus floated for a moment on its own out in
weightlessness like a piece of toast popped
slow-motion from its toaster
the music was Debussy out here in space
the music was actually dead silence
not even a pin drop
which also is interior-most caverns
way way in where no water even drips in an
inverted cone-shape up from the floor and
hooves however light can't be heard
pattering on the loose shale above us

The tunnel fills with laughter
and you are gone except for the memory of you
fired up like an old jalopy from time to time just to see if it
still works

On second thought
maybe I should put a second pair of walking shoes over my
shoulders and take to the open road
the earth pulls away from us so fast as if we're
insufficient conversationalists and it
needs to go where the talk is more enticing

On second thought
the talk here is about as enticing as it gets
a sex-starved alley cat making gurgling
throat sounds as it wails outside my window
clusters of birdsong in tree branches down the street
like a choral patchwork
cloud interpenetrating the leaves

the utter blackness of the night slowly
giving way to day

God God it's such a little space

and we
hunger for mountains

                                                                                  5/24

STORY OUT OF NOWHERE

1

Of course it should be possible to start a
story right here and let it loosen out further and

further until it nearly encompasses just about
everything every love-glance every love-gulp every

gulf as wide as the Atlantic itself between our
very patched selves and perfect God

such as a story about an ant say who
meanders along his Ouspenskyan two dimensions all his

life until one day his vista opens as wide as
double doors on a Renaissance garden

He sees a third dimension by its angular intrusion into his usual two
accompanied by faint zither music and distant

trumpets he undergoes a transformation
appropriate to someone having their

bottom fall out and their sides and top extend
into undreamt-before perceptions you could say

he's left antdom by being so expanded and perhaps that's
true although perhaps just as accurately he's actually

achieved true antdom for the first time in his life not just those
dutiful plodding steps as if on stiff stilts and twitching feelers but now

full inhalation of cosmos and exhalation of illusory self
inhalation and exhalation becoming at some point one

but what do I know
what stars are above me

what wonders await me I have no
idea what my death will be or where my

life is taking me what double doors onto what
Renaissance gardens or post-Renaissance German

Expressionist labyrinth pathways with looming
angular walls and dizzying inclines yet at

heart it is the same story that could if fated
unroll from here and embrace by its

purest wit and Godly wisdom even the most
nonchalant player with hands in pockets and cigarette

dangling from raw lips eyes slits smoke curling up in
front of his or her face in which suddenly

he or she sees more than expected
the double doors to his or her life suddenly

swing open and why not

onto a long beach that extends into another

territory altogether where people greet each other from the
deepmost parts of their hearts eyes like delirious

singers whose songs have a lilting simplicity that
catches everyone in their nets and each

exchange is from the
fullest bellow and aria of the

glorious human heart in full splendor and yet
simplicity itself a

gesture so fine made with human hand the poignant
sound of a voice long-distance telling its

tale of woe and visceral recognitions
the sexual perplexities as if giant looming

silhouettes on specially built platforms like
ancient shaman ceremonies involving

trance and words to a
new revelation to

take place with every
encounter we can

ever expect to have
and yet each one astonishingly

the same and at the same time unique

The ant goes back to its hill and
wonders if it was dreaming or if it is

presently dreaming whether the
real is the universe turned inside out so the

silver backside of it shows and it
no longer reflects the same old

grimaces and smiles or whether it is really just
this one so hard to actually define and seemingly most

friendly to those who plunge into the fire of it
headfirst to find its silken pathways

extending from the bottoms of their feet
tended and watched over by the

long gaze of God

2

Episode without precedent or antecedent
afloat on the sea of it
bobbing happily to itself so self-contained and
self-sufficient as if
nothing but itself mattered
life flowing out both ends into tumultuous nothingness

starting abruptly and ending abruptly

someone coming into a room chattering and going
out of it again leaving dead silence behind

us fidgeting with things or rearranging papers
or simply thunderstruck and inert at the
explosiveness of the story while it was here
its perfect nouns and verbs moving it along
its adjectives giving it color both
local and cosmic

starshine on the forehead of the girl from the
mountains or dune-burn from the rough
caravan leader who knows how to speak to
camels better than to men

and so the episode lives in the air like a
spark from a night fire thrown up in the
blackness like a jinn's spangle bright gold then
gone

but while it's alive it has the dimension of
palaces with thousands of rooms and
elongated corridors and formal and informal
gardens out windows and archways in which

at all hours trysts and dramatic turns of
event take place the breaking of
horses and the submission of wills and the
freeing of spirits to fly on their own wings not like drunk

moths to the flame of the sun but like serious

water birds capable of transcontinental
travel into
continuous oceans of sky

auroral wonders

3

For no sooner does a story start its journey
out of the dark step by ant-step across the
blank page of space it also begins to
reverberate outward and inward in geometric
dimensions and someone pulls out her
mother-of-pearl combs and yellow hair
tumbles to her shoulders and distant horses
whinny maybe Mongols maybe not in which case

ten hours later there's no city at all no
hair tumbling framed by no window there for
centuries until ten hours ago

The story unwinds across faces and their anguishes
it's hinged in the oddest places and suddenly whole
unexpected panels open out in which for example
the uncle from St. Petersburg who was supposed to
inherit the farm and its two thousand acres has a
fit with eyes rolling up into head clutching tablecloth with
all the silver and china crashing to the floor and he's

under the table dead and the farm takes
wing and sails over the mountains to a distant
province giving sustenance to the yellow-haired
woman from before who happened to
escape the chopping blows by feigning death under a
haystack *etcetera etcetera* it's

booming along with rattles and bells of its
own completely out of the
storyteller's control in that the storyteller wanted to tell a
tale of a family of saintly dwarves living inside a tree

and suddenly we're in Russia where Chekhov for example
told stories that glittered with a life all their
own incomparably sober and self-contained

4

A tree grew from the air
and turned into a bird

A stone rose from a stream
and stepped onto shore

Water drops fell to earth
and each one flew off as a fly

The sun lifted its bulk
and its writhing tentacles caught fire

The oceans abruptly sat up
and creatures fell out of their deeps

Yet now when you look at the sky the
tree the stone the stream rushing noisily between the

hard toes of the rocks
everything's back to normal

Or is it?

5

The narrative flow as they say
out of the mouth of the first to speak
at the dawn of the ages

but there was not one who was first
but many all talking at once from
time immemorial

talking as normally as you or me
saying gravelly things to further the
narrative flow saying *"Don't go too near that
waterfall!"* or *"We saw a mastodon stuck in a
bog this morning — Oh boy God be praised —
we'll eat for a week!"*

Or far more complicated things like
"She entered the place as the sun was setting in a

purple blaze like a meteor entering the sea
and the air seemed to notice her"

The narrative flow till the end of time on the
lips of everyone

The end

6

The story of the man with no toes who composed
    his odes on the run

The story of the twenty schoolgirls who circled
    a hill until it disappeared

The story of the cat who dived into a cardboard
    box to investigate the void and came out
    a Buddhist

The three-cornered hat that refused to revolt
    in the general throng that would later
    become the status quo worth
    revolting against and so
sat on a head in obstinate refusal until it
    sprouted feathers and ended as the
    master of *haute couture*

The story of the three magpies looking down at the
    dead knight sprawled at the base of their tree

The story of the first people envisioning the
   last people and laughing at the
   joke as their campfire flickers in the dark

The story of the woman who brought food to
   orphans and came home to find her
   home had been transformed into a
   celestial piano playing tunes to
   transport her to Paradise

The story of tragic lovers each in their respective waterfalls
   signaling to each other through the downrushing
   cascades in a glittering blur of longing

The story of the end of stories and giant
   cracks appear in our walls and our feet become
   flat and our windows black over

The story of the beginning of stories as a newborn
   baby looks around and seems to be perfectly
   at ease and the enlightened
   master of her domain

Each thought-bubble an epic with horseback
   armies and attendant angels

Each phrase we speak conscious or not
a haiku that encapsulates both the
season and the moment of epiphany as
surely as the settling down through the air of a gnat on a
newly fallen plum on gray pavement

Each entrance into night or exit into day
the delicious unfolding of a parchment of
stories whose starlight proceeds from
actual stars and whose

main characters are aspects of our
own hearts going past each other and
recognizing each face from childhood on
each story accompanied by distant
chimes and a gong the size of Manhattan

Each denouement only the ashes a
strange new Phoenix rises out of
trailing the vocabulary words of the entire
story in a heartbeat that
we are about to embark on having

started before the creation of the universe
just as we're about to
open our lips in
praise of the simplest notion
and in anticipation of the
most distant galactic recognition

coming as close to us as our breaths are
or even closer

coming as close to us as our deaths are
only a pause in the story
that resumes again
like an illuminated manuscript caught fire in a

shaft of light

in which we too exist
transformed into

the purest story of God's unfolding blessing on all of us

amen

                                                                                                 6/28

THE SOUND OF EARTH'S ROTATION

There's the sound of the earth's rotation as it
swings past space friction a kind of
squeak audible in peoples' speech patterns to the
most attuned ear or audible in the upturn at the
end of birds' song-lines the last notes
ascending in a disintegrating splatter

or in the way lovers while getting to know each
other in the way that used to be called
courting anticipate what each other might
say or anticipate a kind of crescendo like an
orchestra in unison holding a long note extra
long as emphasis for an epiphanic
emotion that seems to go on forever and actually does

The sound of the earth's rotation in the roar of
hungry lions around feeding time a sound of
leonine rasping large things scraping together like
big iron machinery

or on the other hand a sound completely at the
other end of the stress scale of water
lapping on the shore of a Polynesian island the
hushed insistence a long lead-up to a
momentary pause before an even longer
sizzle as it slides back down again into the
next arising wave

Perhaps I'm only recounting random things with

sound as being part of the earth's
rotation when it's not really the noise a giant
celestial body makes as it moves round its
axis in the dark with one half in the
light which may not make any sound at all audible to our
ears as an actual sound as such but still all the

eerie and varied activities upon the earth as it
sails so free and easy round its
slightly tilted axis might yet be described as
contributing to the overall
ecumenically rich and eclectically inclusive
symphony of that sound

              6/30

THE PUPPETS

The puppets all demand equal opportunity
they gaze with blinkless eyes and dry mouths

they are all about to speak without first
clearing their throats

their horses have all galloped away without them
some are merrier than others

some have tragic secrets while others wish they could
perfect their whistles

they have all wished they could swing in trees
their sense of smell is defective

The puppets sit in rows and gaze at the ceiling
like newborn babies or very old people waiting for

death though puppets never die
they begin where everyone else leaves off

they have stories to tell but no bodies to
tell them with

many have fallen and many have risen
but no one has come from a larger family than

the puppet family
roses mimic their continual freshness

light mimics their unstinting expression whichever
it happens to be happy or sad wise or stupid

speed is not their forte their forte is
silence and perseverance and a kind of

stoic strength
you have to hand it to a puppet

while we wax and wane in perpetual
idiosyncrasy puppets are steadfast and have

infinite patience
and no problem saying farewell

and a relaxed attitude about greeting
though deaf they seem attentive

though blind they look interested and even at times
amazed

though dead they will never be alive
unless Pinocchio is their prophet sent to

lead them to their true natures

The god of puppets is the same God as for everyone

7/4

THE PRAYER OF THE ANGELS

The prayer of the angels
that makes blue tips on flames dance golden
and windows open in arc'd rainbows
flattens earth's curvature when we're
standing on it so we won't fear sliding off into the sky

The prayer of the angels as they thread through matter
drip down with candle wax
roll with rubber tires along asphalt highways
hum along telephone wires clarifying electric garble into
sweet human conversation

The prayer that sustains them in their rounds
across the arctic and below the equator
is murmured equally on the lips of the newborns of every species
as they open their eyes for the first time
of humans when they see an ocean for the first time
of surgeons when they press their sharp
scalpels on a live person for the first time
when a duck takes her ducklings to water for the first time
when humans make sexual love for the first time

And soft bells tumble from clouds and fall
as slowly as time itself into seas like eyelids that open
just enough to let them enter

echoing unheard

7/6

SOME OF THE HEAVEN ELEMENT

Some of the heaven element fell into the earth element
scattering hot red sparks in all directions like termites
and the cool blue block of it sat on a hill
steaming a kind of chalky nimbus out of which
strange shadows leapt
people approached with caution first the curious children
the sniffing cats the yapping dogs then the
officials driving up in fleets of cars

It sat on that hill with an attitude of inviolability and
somehow no one objected
there were four sides and a top to it one couldn't
tell about the bottom no one
dared touch it not even the
children

On the four sides and top however you could
sort of see pictures like cloud-shifting images
swiftly passing against a blinding pellucid blue
and if you leaned real close (the scientists and
theosophists noticed this first) you could hear a
kind of singing

But the images were disconcerting they were
bawdy even lewd almost one might say
devilish images of gigantic couplings and earth-shakings
forests defoliated and even deforested
people skewered and pilloried darkness and
even greater darkness

until the cube began to emit salty brine like
tears running in small rivulets down that hill

Everyone stood back took a few steps
back afraid to look

The cube purged itself then of all pictures
and in their place there was first
stillness and nothing then gradually
a kind of golden point which got
bigger and bigger even finally
going off the cube entirely exceeding
its cubical dimensions and transparently
hovering in the air

No one who was there
was exempt

from that golden air

7/21

ZIGZAG ROAD

The zigzag road to the summit
eaten by roosters
the egg of the sun cracked on the horizon's edge
light liquefied and coming this way
silver horses of various sizes with eyes like rainbows
turned on their sides and manes like clouds
these horses of where-are-you-going rather than
where-have-you-been
their whinnies wake up the night but no one's home
and everyone gets up scratching
the chemical elements like electric lights on a single line
each one a different color

You've been-here-before but you didn't know it yet
and you're-here-now but you've almost begun to forget
yet yellow houses in a row up the steep hillside remind you of
the words of a song probably in Chinese
and not from another lifetime and not from this
this one's a forward-moving arrow whose tip has been
dipped in the blood of the sun

An elegant man in tuxedo and painted face
has just announced the next performance
something from Brazil
with no dancing
dancing is left to the bears each with a
cosmos of buzzing flies around it
and the corners of newspapers lifted delicately by the wind

Somehow this poem began in the middle instead of at the
beginning and I have the distinct feeling it will end
near the beginning instead of near the end

Out the window a Ferris-wheel is turning
or it may be the sound the traffic or even
the river the rush-hour of salmon is making its
annual up-river migration on
it's a sound you feel you could disappear in
water over rocks going at a furious pace
just before opening out into navigable
ocean with its presidential whales and secretarial dolphins

I love the anything-can-happen feeling mainly because
anything can and does
and already has

God bless us all at the beginning middle and end
for without us the rain might have one less to fall on
one destiny less to befall on

one less answer to His call

7/31
(*after 60th birthday*)

THE FORTIETH

The fortieth has arrived fortieth poem fortieth foray
forward in this book populated by
people with no shoes and bad haircuts
singing slightly off key because of their
inner complexity

I've seen them in the distance through
high powered binoculars as well as
so close up as to be x-ray

They are maps of cosmos not tattooed but actually
embodied
light falls across their channels and sinks
deep into their pores
but it's useless to describe them because they are always
elsewhere
we can look high and low for them and they
won't be there

People enter the picture and then leave it
sunlight or moonlight flooding the empty frame
they take their promises with them since they
made them in the first place and they were
never truly mine
like tickets aboard a luxury ocean liner but the
ocean liner's a movie set flat plywood affair you'd fall
right into the water if you entered

They take their strange courage and meekness

their ultimate vulnerability

They take their forward dreams and their backwards ones
the ones that reach them from the future like crawling surf
the ones that suck them back from the past
like a vacuum that exists because their
present state may not be full enough to provide
weight and ballast

                                                                              8/6

TREE OF LIFE

The tree that is the tree of life has three branches
and millions of leaves and on each branch
a bridge and on each bridge multitudes of
crickets making their itchy music and listening to
replies from far and near

The tree of life sprouts from our hearts with
roots that go down past our toes into the
earth under our feet earth of bone and smoke
earth of glad song and openings

The tree of life swings on its own branches on which are hung
the portraits in fine detail and exquisite color
of everyone ever alive alive now and alive to come
a never-ending display of astonished and
astonishing faces each with open eyes and
words of great beauty even the
beastliest among them

The tree of life grows upward with each
planetary breath and its reflection can be
seen in the ocean of space
where suns and moons and planets rotate with the
swimming serenity of whales

Shade from the tree of life is sparse but it
broods like a gentle mother over each
one of us and rays of light break through in
ribbony bands that spell words of

elemental wisdom and comfort

Do not take an axe to it
do not take it down for any reason
don't carve your name on it or look greedily at its
lumber

Its rings go deep into the center of the world
you can read its age by the
amount of life you have lived

Take one leaf and let that be your
shield your parasol and your grave

8/7

THE WINE OF LIFE

She tasted the wine of life but spat it out
it was bitter it had death in it
she drank water but it only made her thirsty
the wine with its dark core which reached the
tips of her senses
and flung open the house windows and
swept the walk of leaves in one stroke

but it had death in it a bitter aftertaste or
foretaste so she
spat it out

She chose a slim unknown bottle with a clear
slightly greenish liquid in it and felt it was
sunshine in glass or stoppered positivity with no blemish
so she drank and drank and it was as she
thought and she looked through positive sunshine eyes
and banished death
and drove past her life which would have
taken many turns for the worse and one
turn so far beyond what was best so
far beyond her highest hopes for happiness
going down a rapids and becoming beclouded in the
spray of it taken for mad and written off as
lost but on her face and in her heart
no stream of water trickling but
rather glorious tons of catapulting hydraulic energy that
would have placed her next to death or around death itself with its
clown white face on a black face

its black face on a white
its perfect teeth and blazing eyes

And it would have driven her too close to the edge

but the sun rises and sets for it

for the mere taste of it

the sun rises and sets

8/7

ANCIENT CITY

There was an ancient city that rolled up a hill
and down again
and on it were assembled the women and men
of antiquity
horse carts full of hay and giant jugs made of
clay and olive groves with wrangling branches
already millennia old and olives the size of
grapes and grapes the size of olives
green-gray in the rays of the setting sun

Now they're all in ruins
the walls are fallen and the people are gone
but the olive groves still grow with their
green-gray olives
the hay-cats of today squeak their wooden wheels as
they go up the hills and down laden down
no boy eyes girl by highway wall
at least not from antiquity

and this poem struggles on to the end
in spite of its tendency to fall into ruins before it's
even had the chance to sing a somber song
that lifts over the ruined walls among scattered
stones and graves of unmarked bones

through the whistling sky
where these ruins lie

8/9

IN AN AIR OF NO IMPORTANCE

In an air of no importance a sudden
gale may blow
in a sound of utter blandness a crash

Through a millionth door of nondescript allure
a full-color universe may heave into view
and take you into its texture and deep
within its weave
to hold ritual objects and things made of glass

Or you suddenly find yourself on a desert island
with a sky full of unidentified flying objects
and a single rod good for flushing out beach crabs

A small light may grow into a giant conflagration
an offhand comment grow into an unintended squabble
a glance open oceans in the air between you
filled with floating icebergs thousands of feet deep

a shout enough to ring through iron canyons
a call bring back a soul from the edge of the abyss
at the last moment when this world with all its magnetism
is pulling away and the breath of the next is
brushing against her lips

Nothing is final except finality
and the metamorphosis of cane into syrup infinite
the transformation of bug into bird
the capitulation of army into ant colony

war into blood bank
heart into field of bright orange poppies
inebriating the passersby with song

                                                                              8/12

LIGHTFINGERED LOUIE

He leaves clues on lip-edges of cups
fingerprints on doorways
swans strangled on their ponds
horses blinded in their stalls
owls headless as they hoot at the moon
silence tilted on its side
footprints up one side of a void
walking away on their own down the
other
conversations hanging in midair
lies on the lips of their liars
one face for sunlight another for night
miles of manuscripts unread
moonlight filtering through the windows of ruins
goats in haystacks bleating for their nannies

He puts two bright boats on the high seas and
lets them drift

He is and isn't both simultaneously and forever

He's the perfect double agent
gone again now again
Lightfingered Louie

He's got us by the eyebrows
and he won't let go

8/15

GOLDEN GLOBULES

The melting of golden globules
slithering down a sparkling stem into a
white pool

Figures in armor stand in the moonlight
listening to the crackling making the
prayer of their lifetimes before the
dawn

and a white bird goes out like a lunar boomerang
in a wide arc
coming back with the
dark nothingness that is in their hearts and
reading it back to them whose
silver eyes click open and shut

The moonlight splinters
the light disappears
except the light in their eyes

NON-RHETORICAL CAT-YOWL

Our female housebound cat listens at the screen door in the night
as an unseen tomcat goes trolling with his gargled
voice of sex-pain out in the alley
in the moonlight

Unknown world to her out there
serpents bigger than highways
slithering down out of the hills to curl
round the city red eyes flashing
the ocean's in-and-out breathing way off to the right
tiny people marveling at the boats on its back
while deep inside Russians in a
submarine no longer gasp for air
floating in brine with expressionless faces in their nuclear casket

Fantasy and reality doing their
best to intermingle so one wears the
face of the other and the other wears the
face of the one
and when we reach out to touch we're never quite
sure which one of the two we're touching

Someone somewhere is waking from millennial sleep
head above the clouds
heart filled with radical aromas
eyesight so clear fragmented herds of night disperse into
flying goose flocks in perfect V's that flow through the day

and everyone's name appears with itinerant

blessings across his heart screen
or she dips her saintly hand into a jug of water and
pulls out pearls

All of this sizzling in our cat's ruminations of wonder
as the tomcat grows silent out of
exhaustion or fulfillment we'll never know which

Oh there he is again
with his absolutely non-rhetorical yowl

Our sedate black cat alert on her haunches with
twitching ears

ponders

8/20

PHRASES

One day a tree said, *"OK, I'm stumped!"*
The whole valley laughed

A rock flung itself at someone
then hunkered down on the road

A wind blew quickly around a tree
then said *"Phew! I'm winded!"*

A cliff whispered *"Drop over sometime"*
then laughed at the old joke

A tree fell in the middle of a forest
and said *"Was that really me making all that noise?"*

An an echo echo said said Hello Hello would would you you
mind mind repeating repeating that that?

A tomb said *"Silent as a tomb"* silently to itself
then remained silent

Up said to itself *"Nowhere to go but up"*

Down said to itself *"Nowhere to go but down"*

The road not taken remained untaken

A merry-go-round stopped going round and
stopped being merry

A dead end dropped dead at the end
and so shall we

Little silver slippers dance at the margin
at the thought of eternity

heartbeats of beatitude
sprout wings of bliss

dawn breaks into a zillion particles and a zillion waves
just like this

8/25

SPECTACULAR SANDWICHES

The ray of light that fell on the head of the boastful betrayer
became a palace with elegant courtyards and splashing fountains

and birdsong echoing in the corridors
and he looked up from his usual pit and saw everywhere

the glory in a fern the splendor of space how everything that
enters it is holy and alone

everything that leaves it is on its journey to the King
his own face became the earth's reflection in the clear pool

of his own being and
clouds passed across his bright turquoise sky

spelling out in carefully vanishing letters
the momentary scriptures of his life

wrongs and attitudes fell off him like dead skin
for there is nowhere to go if our walls have no doors

and our breath is a dead end if the
fine-meshed body around it is made of

stone instead of wiry gossamer God's Light can penetrate
running electricity along every gesture

to illuminate the faces of our beloved friends
who gather in that garden around that fountain

with their spectacular sandwiches

8/27

EVERYTHING

Everything's in sequence for the one with a single focal point
everything's simultaneous for the one whose focal point floats

The spectacular and tragic train crash in Minsk
takes place after the train leaves the station an hour earlier
or else simultaneous with its departure
as well as simultaneous with the blond Brazilian trapeze artist's skill
as she floats in gold sequins through the air

as well as with the extinction of the last dinosaurs and
Madame de Stael's momentary indigestion from
a tri-cornered open-faced cream cheese sandwich at exactly 3 p.m.
on a Sunday

Or else in militarily exact regimen of sequence
in a universe that is always bursting forward in time
like the cicada bursting out of its exoskeletal adolescent
shell leaving it clinging upside-down and almost transparent on a
rose leaf

And yet the experience of things normally as we
all sit simultaneously on the side of my
4 a.m. bed in Philadelphia on the 28th of August Year 2000
longitude and latitude whatever under the stars
as well as simultaneously with events
invisible to our eyes at present and
inaudible to our ears

is things in sequence

first *this* happens then *that* follows and finally
this takes place

But such a love that is tangible from actually
nowhere at all

crowds out all earthly distractions both in time and out

and God's love seeps up like a silvery steam through the floor
as well as simultaneously

drifting down from the golden tapestry of the stars
onto our heads

                                                                            8/28

LIGHT ENTERS THE ROOM

> *like light turns to crystal when the water moves*
> — Ed Roberson

1

Light enters the room without feet or hands
a quizzical expression on its face

It flows around everything equally around the
chairs and tables the ivory carvings and Victorian

inkstand the body of a man in khaki stretched
out on the floor behind the writing desk the ruby hilted

dagger in his back the open book the billowing
window curtains the window ledge wide enough to

sit on and continues flowing to the corners and
ceiling in the instant of its arrival deftly

fingering (without hands) each delicate and
precious thing as well as each thick lumbering

thing in the room each gnat around the
lamplit circle of yellowish light around the

crinkles in the corners of the corpse's eyes and
mouth his perfect inertness bathed now in

totally external light no way of knowing what
light or darkness lay inside him too late to

increase himself in any more illumination than
what he had at the moment of truth when the

ruby-handled dagger hit home his facial
expression the last lively thing as

quizzical as the light that illumines the
room he is now in forever the

light sitting perfectly still at all points
equally and watching

2

But why a corpse in all this light?
When it should be a cause for celebration
light capable of celebrating itself through
interrupted flow (flashing) or increase (brilliance
upon brilliance) rushing everywhere at once
rollercoastering over knobs and protuberances
with equal diffusion in a wink
in which a new ecstatic affirmation might be affirmed
a child born to a childless couple
a ruthless murderer apprehended
which brings us to this once live object sprawled on the
splendid oriental carpet from Turkmenistan
an eminent archeologist who spent decades exploring

the Valley of the Kings and cracked the hieroglyphic
code at Teotihuacan
now cruelly dead in all this light in this
halting fiction I'm inaugurating out of the
lamplit brightness of a blank notebook page
without particularly intending anything by it
except to indicate light's pure democracy
and utter neutrality to everything and anything it
comes across flows across like a
waterfall cascade pursuing its
destination which is never it final one
light's origin and destination actually
one and the same

3

Unwrapping gold foil from Hershey's Chocolate Nuggets
sipping iced Nestea from the motel glass

in Burlington Vermont surrounded in the black and
rainy night by heavily wooded mountains under the

starless sky in the crickety quiet distant
traffic whistling by light on this porch

dim and uneventful
wondering how this poem with dead body came

about and where it's going I don't know any more than
the gas station attendant down the road who may

never have read a single poem in his whole
sad life or who may have a back room full of

secret manuscripts the epic of the human race he
flops into a chair back there each night to write

and he's up past the Renaissance by now with
axle grease under his fingernails and in the

creases of his palms that if read correctly by the
right gypsy might reveal whether he'll

finish his perfect epic in perfect heroic couplets
before he dies or tragically not

going each morning back to the pumps with a
greasy red cloth for taking off radiator caps

the poetic genius of Full Serve in a backwards cap
the light having exploded inside everyone of us

like cosmic starfish of molecular expansion
to the very ends of our senses the very sensitive

tips of our *sensorium* in continual flashes
picking up the conversations of saints long dead

or to come long after we're gone
light in the shape of a burning shoe hurled skyward

light in the shape of a shining coil intertwined with a

glittering counter-coil inside

light that lights up the darkest face with a bluish light
light of unutterable happiness and delight

light the exact shape of this motel porch on earth tonight
glowing peachy pinkish in the deep black starless night

within which I write

                                                    8/2-9/1

THE SKY IS BLUE

The sky is blue
the road is red
the night is black
the heart is blue

or a kind of blue-green
colors grow by the side of the road
the air is a rainbow in black and white
a horse just entered a coral rose

an orange fire broke out
an orange fire bloomed
a dark red rust-colored fire just died
everything is filed in its proper place

a thousand little multi-colored specks just flew
by the iron yard sitting in the sunlight dull gray
and black and huge patch brown with a
flesh-colored old human being brought down
brought down by the blues

the colors of his face cast by the lights in his soul
brought down brought down by the
blues

or the light blue-greens
shuffling sad through the black earth
heart like an ember barely aglow
there's a horse somewhere a

coral rose that could
take him away to a land of light
I've seen the coming of endless night

the sky is blue
the road is red
the night's on fire
the heart's on fire

the sky is blue
the road is red
the night is black
the heart is blue

                                            9/14

BANQUET

Saint Francis had an itch but he
did not scratch it for that would divert
God's destiny in the world

Caesar saw the bloody swords in the sky above their
grim determined faces
but did not shun his forward steps
even glad to be relieved of a power that
was not his

Saint Catherine of Genoa felt the rough-edged
pebble underfoot and cast her eyes heavenward
not avoiding the pinch and a tiny trail of
her blood wrote out a legible sentence in the
dirt ants followed for
ten years afterwards

The invisible ribs around the world from
pole to pole the encircling bands of
angels at the equator swimming continuously around
my own eyeblinks as they
close to the outside world and simultaneously
open inwardly with a more
stellar amazement

The banquet to which everyone is invited
but only a handful come
or to which everyone comes but only a
handful are invited

The first people must have been saints as well
perfectly formed and capable of the subtlest
communication of thought in rhythmic
chant from heart to heart

One refused to scratch an itch

another died standing up with arms outstretched

another danced and danced until he dropped

9/15

ANGELS HOLDING SMALL MIRRORS

Angels holding small mirrors
wearing blue shoes
but angels have no feet and
need none as they drift out top-story
windows of the tallest buildings like the
steam from teapot spouts in lazy
ribbony *alifs* into the cloudless turquoise of the sky

and yet your eyes fill with tears and so do
mine at the same time for we are

somehow far from such visions although our
hearts are pools in which such
visions could be reflected even if
upside-down and bears could also

gaze into the water hoping for trout or
small children in bright bathing suits to
leap in unafraid in the knowledge that the
water will hold them as a
mother's hand does above the rocks of
misfortune

So that we go from the top of the sky where these
blue-shoed angels are to the
bottom of the lake where sweet kicking
children bubble up with bluish faces of
angels though their feet have the requisite

numbers of toes and their hearts are
already in heaven

9/21

THE MOMENT OF LOSING CONSCIOUSNESS

We don't remember the moment of losing consciousness
we only experience gaining it again
if at all
imagine returning to consciousness say as a
huge bird and we think
hey last I knew I was a 60 year old white guy lying in a
bed trying to go to sleep and suddenly I'm in a
nest on a branch at the top of a mountain under
low clouds wind 10 degrees north by north-west and I'm
lifting off having just untucked my head from under my
right wing and I
wonder next time I fall asleep just what if anything I
wake up as because being a bird as I am now
my entire conscious life is certainly
wonderful but I wouldn't want to wake up as say a
kind of solemn but conscious rock or tree even though
being a tree has a certain leafy allure

Then we sleep again and what whole world
claims us while we're gone and what will we
do when destiny decrees it's the last falling out of this
present consciousness and the next coming-to is in
not this world but the next as whatever in the
next world that may
happen to be I hope it's not a burning house a
bug the size of New York a lake of flaming tar or
a book with too many crammed-together black
sentences almost unreadable but if
read would prove me doomed to an

eternity of something I'd just as soon not
wake up to ever instead of say

a lagoon with silvery laughter stroking a
cat or two under the shade of large
elephant leaves in the shape of actually
my original self totally and completely at
ease and awake to each
nuance of spirit and body as they
glide in a stationary stance through time and
space with a plain but beatific
smile forever on my face

                                                         9/21

DINNER BELL

A friend has decided he wants to write about death
though the great lotus opens inside him
with its thick white petals like an
upholstered coffin and its
sweet smell

A coal black horse waits saddled but riderless at the door
facing east

as we ate breakfast at the International House of Pancakes
I told him each of us has a life-span's allotted provision
be it lobster thermodor or bowls of rice
and when it finally runs out for us by divine decree at birth
we die

The coal-black horse at the door munches bright green grass
the bright green grass eats water and sunlight
inside us cells eat what's necessary for their
sustenance and salvation
the ocean eats the shore
the earth swings in an elliptical orbit in a big bite
taken out of heaven

The death gong sounds for the dinner bell
we look at our fellow diners

They arrive one by one from everywhere
and sit down to eat

SHY HEMLOCKS BRASH NIAGARAS

for Abd al-Hakim Murad

Shy hemlocks brash Niagaras
natural things embraced with such articulate

consciousness
we walk by streams hearing their gurgle as they

repeat the Creator's Name over and over
cranes fly by in their rhapsodic formations

geese honking glory among the cloudless
molecules of the sky each molecule a

communications center where God's manifest
decrees are sent from one noisy

interior to another
light rays zigzagging everywhere charting their

lateral and diagonal alchemical formulas
transforming uniform darkness into distinct

shades of the rainbow outlined by incantatory lights
a dervish divesting himself of his own plaintive shadows

as he walks down the road noticing even the lowliest
pebbles are hushedly singing not only to each

other but to the bare soles of his feet
each glance is a mouth each glance is an ear

emitting and taking in the most articulate designations
leading back by elegant grammar of each manifest thing

to the Unmanifest Source Who has spoken
each thing into being

flame tips with scarlet lips that
glow in the dark as they speak

windows that gaze onto landscapes of boundless joy
hills that actually sing as they frolic valleys that stretch out on their

quivering backs greening themselves and humming in the solemnly throbbing sun

God One the Universe One in the
wise mathematics of this singular song

9/30 – Chicago

OCEAN VIEW

I look out at the ocean the ocean looks back at me
it comes closer and closer but never quite reaches me
gray green water fringe of flashing gray froth
rapping trillions of nervous white fingertips on shore
then giving up and sliding under
impatience held by God's magnet to purest oceanic form
blank gray sky granulated beige sand
fine purple sea threads chipped creamy shells
boom swish symphonic sound carried to ears by whispering wind

If there were an anthology of the ocean's best waves
wouldn't they all be in it?

Seagulls perch on stiff legs
ragged faces into the wind

Are we near the beginning or end
of the chronological order of the waves?

Sky becomes ocean ocean becomes shore shore becomes
this conscious bodily presence I am sitting cross-legged
as water incessantly crests and slaps down

The mind gone

                                                               10/5

THE FORBEARANCE OF CATS

I Think the cats are the only ones who can
stand my snoring
I'm asleep so as far as I'm concerned I
sleep like a baby
but I've noticed a wrecking crew sometimes will put
difficult structures next to my bed at night
and in the morning they're rubble
and when the sound track was lost recently for a
nature program about The Rhinoceros they
set up microphones next to my bed and said "*sweet dreams*"

The sad thing is my father snored horribly
audible throughout my childhood nights keeping my
long-suffering mother awake in her
twin bed having to dose herself with sleeping pills for over 50 years to
sleep and I inwardly hated it and vowed I'd
never snore but apparently
break that vow to smithereens every night as soon as
I'm asleep

I sleep in the basement bedroom of our house
my wife's on the top floor and we've
slept this way for a dozen years or so of our
twenty plus year perfectly happy marriage

When we go on trips and have to sleep in motels she brings
a little pillbox of ear plugs though anyone
else (such as our kids) may suffer a full night of
sleeplessness

I do sometimes wake myself up but not often
cracks have appeared in the walls and the
paint's hanging off my bedroom furniture in strips
car engines are modeled on my few
quiet periods between eruptions
ethnologists are writing scholarly papers citing me as
evidence for ogres

But the cats must think I'm their mother or something
one of them occasionally sleeps at the foot of my bed with me
calmly rising and falling with the general upheaval
sometimes purring along with me
which I've noticed on a few occasions when I
suddenly wake up possibly having
snorted especially loudly or made some other
unearthly noise hardly appropriate to a
human mortal that reaches way in past my
sleeping consciousness and
wrenches me awake

                                                                   10/6

A HIGH NOTE

A high note

a whole country can come into being
as if floating on cloud

wide boulevards
trees of impossible foliage and deep shade
angelic wagons filled with giant fruits
glistening in a pink sun
dusty pink sunlight touched with bronze
drifting onto everything

We could enter this country in a wink
interior layers of viscera
everyone especially halo'd
from the dark cardiac muscle
clenching and unclenching its metrical ocean

We could stand up in it if we dared
normal existence flaking away
a tumble of wood blocks and tin whistles

It's more than just a matter of alternating light and shade
ancient ventricular cathedral
deep echoes in the antechambers
voices among columns melodiously singing

one face facing the interface of the sky

10/7

THE PLUM OF THE MOMENT

The plum of the moment perches on the thimble of love
it's delicious but hard to attain though its

juice flow all around us
the thimble holds the ocean which can be heard

sloshing in its tiny shell
echoes of waves and deep-down currents

inside this smallest of containers
even Saturnian orbits as they squeak in outer space

also in that thimble and
zebra mothers as their rickety newborn colts get up

to begin to suckle
out in the whispering tundras

but there that sweet plum sits
waiting to be plucked

the thimble to be tipped so its
small ocean flow oceanward

and join some major waves
horizon melting into sky

and all its boatmen falling into swoons of joy
as they skim its glistening sheen

light of the sky reflecting from its face
love's horizon melting into space

10/8

SPARKS

Sparks dancing in multiple patterns inside the light
each life alive

Mongolian lips and African eyes and cheeks of flame
each body a variable substitute

for the body of light suspended in the primordial
ray of light full of

affable gestures and innocent facial expressions and
words of worry and words of praise

exchanged in the air and returning through
meticulous grammatical tubes of language to the original light

Each one of us a cosmos whose oceans are
suds of light washing eternally around the

erodable continents whose shifting shores draw the
profiles of our human forms in sand before

sucking them back into eternal bright
waves of light

In each of our eyes sighted or sightless
stars of light

In each of our faces mirrors reflecting back the
fullest dictionaries of light possible from each of whose

specific lexiconical definitions burst full
fountains of light whose texts flow freely

into every corner of darkness
which is actually only the

flip side of light

                                                      10/8

ABOUT THE AUTHOR

Born in 1940 in Oakland, California, Daniel Abdal-Hayy Moore's first book of poems, *Dawn Visions*, was published by Lawrence Ferlinghetti of City Lights Books, San Francisco, in 1964, and the second in 1972, *Burnt Heart/Ode to the War Dead*. He created and directed *The Floating Lotus Magic Opera Company* in Berkeley, California in the late 60s, and presented two major productions, *The Walls Are Running Blood*, and *Bliss Apocalypse*. He became a Sufi Muslim in 1970, performed the Hajj in 1972, and lived and traveled throughout Morocco, Spain, Algeria and Nigeria, landing in California and publishing *The Desert is the Only Way Out*, and *Chronicles of Akhira* in the early 80s (Zilzal Press). Residing in Philadelphia since 1990, in 1996 he published *The Ramadan Sonnets* (Jusoor/City Lights), and in 2002, *The Blind Beekeeper* (Jusoor/Syracuse University Press). He has been the major editor for a number of works, including *The Burdah* of Shaykh Busiri, translated by Shaykh Hamza Yusuf, and the poetry of Palestinian poet, Mahmoud Darwish, translated by Munir Akash. He is also widely published on the worldwide web: *The American Muslim, DeenPort*, and his own website: www.danielmoorepoetry.com; and poetry blog: www.ecstaticxchange.wordpress.com, among others. He is also currently literary editor for *Seasons Journal* and *Islamica Magazine*. The Ecstatic Exchange Series is bringing out the extensive body of his works of poetry (a complete list of published works on page 2).

POETIC WORKS by Daniel Abdal-Hayy Moore
Published and Unpublished
(many to appear in *The Ecstatic Exchange* Series)

Dawn Visions (published by City Lights, 1964)
Burnt Heart/Ode to the War Dead (published by City Lights, 1972)
This Body of Black Light Gone Through the Diamond (printed by Fred Stone, Cambridge, Mass, 1965)
On The Streets at Night Alone (1965?)
All Hail the Surgical Lamp (1967)
States of Amazement (1970)

Abdallah Jones and the Disappearing-Dust Caper (published by The Ecstatic Exchange/Crescent Series, 2006)
'Ala ud-Deen and the Magic Lamp
The Chronicles of Akhira (1981) (published by Zilzal Press with Typoglyphs by Karl Kempton, 1986)
Mouloud (1984) (A Zilzal Press chapbook, 1995)
Man is the Crown of Creation (1984)
The Look of the Lion (The Parabolas of Sight) (1984)
The Desert is the Only Way Out (completed 4/21/84) (Zilzal Press chapbook, 1985)
Atomic Dance (1984) (am here books, 1988)
Outlandish Tales (1984)
Awake as Never Before (12/26/84) (Zilzal Press chapbook, 1993)
Glorious Intervals (1/1/85) (Zilzal Press chapbook, ?)
Long Days on Earth/Book I (1/28 – 8/30/85)
Long Days on Earth/Book II (Hayy Ibn Yaqzan)
Long Days on Earth/Book III (1/22/86)
Long Days on Earth/Book IV (1986)
The Ramadan Sonnets (Long Days on Earth/Book V) (5/9 – 6/11/86) (Published by Jusoor/City Lights Books, 1996) (Republished as Ramadan Sonnets by The Ecstatic Exchange, 2005)
Long Days on Earth/Book VI (6-8/30/86)
Holograms (9/4/86 – 3/26/87)
History of the World (The Epic of Man's Survival) (4/7 – 6/18/87)
Exploratory Odes (6/25 – 10/18/87)
The Man at the End of the World (11/11 – 12/10/87)

The Perfect Orchestra (3/30 – 7/25/88)
Fed from Underground Springs (7/30 – 11/23/88)
Ideas of the Heart (11/27/88 – 5/5/89)
New Poems (scattered poems, out of series, from 3/24 – 8/9/89)
Facing Mecca (5/16 – 11/11/89)
A Maddening Disregard for the Passage of Time (11/17/89 – 5/20/90)
The Heart Falls in Love with Visions of Perfection (6/15/90 – 6/2/91)
Like When You Wave at a Train and the Train Hoots Back at You (Farid's Book) (6/11 – 7/26/91) (Published by The Ecstatic Exchange, 2008)
Orpheus Meets Morpheus (8/1/91– 3/14/92)
The Puzzle (3/21/92 – 8/17/93)
The Greater Vehicle (10/17/93 – 4/30/94)
A Hundred Little 3-D Pictures (5/14/94 – 9/11/95)
The Angel Broadcast (9/29 – 12/17/95)
Mecca/Medina Time-Warp (12/19/95 – 1/6/96) (Published as a Zilzal Press chapbook, 1996)
Miracle Songs for the Millennium (1/20 – 10/16/96)
The Blind Beekeeper (11/15/96 – 5/30/97) (Published 2002 by Jusoor/Syracuse University Press)
Chants for the Beauty Feast (6/3 – 10/28/97)
You Open a Door and it's a Starry Night (10/29/97 – 5/23/98) (Published by The Ecstatic Exchange, 2009)
Salt Prayers (5/29 – 10/24/98) (Published by The Ecstatic Exchange, 2005)
Some (10/25/98 – 4/25/99)
Flight to Egypt (5/1 – 5/16/99)
I Imagine a Lion (5/21 – 11/15/99) (Published by The Ecstatic Exchange, 2006)
Millennial Prognostications (11/25/99 – 2/2/2000) (Published by the Ecstatic Exchange, 2009)
Shaking the Quicksilver Pool (original title: *The Book of Infinite Beauty*, 2/4 – 10/8/2000) (Published by The Ecstatic Exchange, 2009)
Blood Songs (10/9/2000 – 4/3/2001)
The Music Space (4/10 – 9/16/2001) (Published by The Ecstatic Exchange, 2007)
Where Death Goes (9/20/2001 – 5/1/2002) (Published by The Ecstatic Exchange, 2009)
The Flame of Transformation Turns to Light (99 Ghazals Written in English) (5/14 – 8/21/2002) Published by The Ecstatic Exchange, 2007)
Through Rose-Colored Glasses (7/22/2002 – 1/15/2003) (Published by The Ecstatic Exchange, 2007)

Psalms for the Broken-Hearted (1/22 – 5/25/2003) (Published by The Ecstatic Exchange, 2006)
Hoopoe's Argument (5/27 – 9/18/03)
Love is a Letter Burning in a High Wind (9/21 – 11/6/2003) (Published by The Ecstatic Exchange, 2006)
Laughing Buddha/Weeping Sufi (11/7/2003 – 1/10/2004) (Published by The Ecstatic Exchange, 2005)
Mars and Beyond (1/20 – 3/29/2004) (Published by The Ecstatic Exchange, 2005)
Underwater Galaxies (4/5 – 7/21/2004) (Published by The Ecstatic Exchange, 2007)
Cooked Oranges (7/23/2004 – 1/24/2005 (Published by The Ecstatic Exchange, 2007)
Holiday from the Perfect Crime (1/25 – 6/11/2005)
Stories Too Fiery to Sing Too Watery to Whisper (6/13 – 10/24/2005)
Coattails of the Saint (10/26/2005 – 5/10/2006) (Published by The Ecstatic Exchange, 2006)
In the Realm of Neither (5/14/2006 – 11/12/06) (Published by The Ecstatic Exchange, 2008)
Invention of the Wheel (11/13/06 – 6/10/07)
The Sound of Geese Over the House (6/15 – 11/4/07)
The Fire Eater's Lunchbreak (11/11/07 – 5/19/2008) (Published by The Ecstatic Exchange, 2008)
Sparks Off the Main Strike (5/24/2008 – 1/10/2009)

www.ingramcontent.com/pod-product-compliance
Lightning Source LLC
Chambersburg PA
CBHW020904090426
42736CB00008B/484